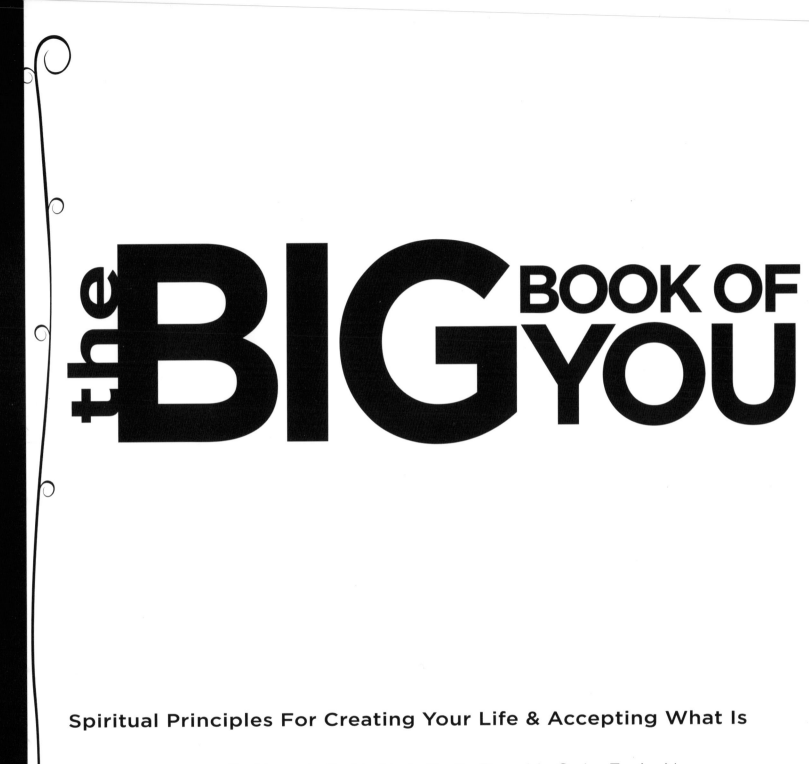

the BIG BOOK OF YOU

Spiritual Principles For Creating Your Life & Accepting What Is

BY JENNIFER MCLEAN

Nascent Press

4533 MacArthur Blvd. #245
Newport Beach, CA 92660

www.McLeanMasterWorks.com

Second Edition McLean MasterWorks Hardcover August 2010

Book design by:
Mary A. Hall, Linda Kamka, Jessica Krewson, Denise Williams and Laura Wathers

ISBN-13: 978-0-9799915-1-6

ISBN-10: 0-9799915-1-X

First Nascent Press hardcover edition November 2008

You are *heavenly*
You are **beautiful**
You are *peaceful*

Photo by: Jennifer McLean

CONTENTS

inner world...

...outer WORLD

Photo by: Jennifer McLean

About The Author

Jennifer McLean is a healer author, speaker, and entrepreneur. She has studied in many disciplines of energy healing therapies and is an accomplished sound healing specialist as well. She has been working in private session with clients from all over the world in person and by phone for more than 18 years offering unique solutions for living a life of ease, grace and balance. She is also a marketer and has written a book called The Credibility Factor. Jennifer's dichotomous experience as a healer and marketing professional afforded her unique insights into the multiple models people use to manage their worlds. This coupled with her lifetime exploration into spiritual challenges and opportunities, and her training as a healer, gave her the tools to write *The Big Book of You*.

Jennifer has contributed chapters and content in Joe Vitale's best-selling book, *The Key,* as well as *The Vision Board Book, and Who do You Think You Are.*, in which she was featured for her unique Body Dialog method of healing. Her contributions included techniques for clearing old, unwanted beliefs, and thoughts that get stuck in the body as emotions that limit expression and human potential. Jennifer is also the host of the renowned Healing With The Masters Seminars, conversing with familiar personalities in the wellness community including, Marianne Williamson, Byron Katie, Neale Donald Walsch, James Redfield, Gregg Braden, Bruce Lipton and so many more.

Jennifer created *The Big Book of You* Thanksgiving weekend 2005 starting with the poetry and it grew from there. As she explored her inner spiritual world and how it works with her outer world, it became clearer that seeming opposites are all contained within the One. The book was born out of that perception and through word and image it juxtaposes all of life. *The Big Book of You* compares and explores the light and the dark of who we are. If we are all one then we are all that we see before us both "good" and "bad." It would be valuable to acknowledge that what we perceive as bad is available to us so that we can release it, knowing it isn't really bad, it just is. The book helps to nudge us in the direction of acknowledging the dark while celebrating the light. Keeping these concepts–dark and light–so close together in the poetry makes it energetically easier to assimilate, find balance and let go. Her products that cover many of the topics found in this book, are available at McLeanMasterWorks.com. You can also experience her coaching and healing work directly through her membership site MasterWorksHealing.com

The Big Book of You compares and explores the light and the dark of who we are. If we are all one then we are all that we see before us both "good" and "bad".

Original Artwork by: Fiona Almeleh

How to Use This Book...Embracing All That Is

The elements that created you are the same components and energy that permeate everything. In fact, I posit that you are the creative force behind your own existence—"it's all you."

The Big Book of You is a work of love that has been formulating for more than two decades. It is a result of my spiritual explorations over that time period, including the learnings, experiences and understandings I have gained. I arrived at the conclusion written here with this artwork: "You are all there is." My journey and spiritual path have led me to this understanding.

The book is divided into two sections. The left-hand pages remind you of all that you are, the light and the dark. The right-hand pages deliver additional spiritual insights and theories I have developed, quotations from renowned individuals from history and modern times as well as further explanations of the ideas about "what you are." You can read the left-hand pages only, or you can read just the right-hand pages; you can also read this as a normal book, from left to right.

We Are All Reflections

I believe that we are each the sum total of our surroundings. We had a hand in creating all that is in our purview, which includes, war, disease, famine, joy, wealth and love. Every time you open your eyes, you witness the reflection of you. You see this reflection in the eyes of your colleagues, friends, neighbors, celebrities, politicians, the cable guy, the grocery clerk, even the IRS guy, and, of course, your beloved pets. Think about this—I am you speaking to you. You are reading this right now because a part of you created the moment to hear about this book. In fact, as I type this, it is a creation in your own mind to receive this information. You had a hand in creating it because you wanted this information, so I am an aspect of you that is looking to experience what you already know. Freaky, huh?

Whether you accept the ideas presented in this book or not, my hope is that, if nothing else, the book will make you think and pause to reflect on your own life, and to remember that you truly are a spectacular being that deserves to find joy, laughter and a fulfilled life, always. There is a divine plan for your life that is beyond your wildest imagination. Also remember that you are part of the all, part of the whole of mankind, including what is created out of the soup of humanness and the habits of humanity. As part of that human infrastructure, you can make a difference. If everything around you is a reflection of you, then you too are part of that reflection, mirroring back to others the energy of perceived "good" and "bad."

So I leave you with a question:

"In the eyes of those around you, how does your reflection contribute to the world?"

Photo by: Jennifer McLean

when we **criticize**

we are ATTACKING

our very own **creation**

it is all YOU

so how could it be

wrong?
wrong? wrong?
wrong?

Why Explore the "Dark"?

When reading the poetry within this book, some have asked, "Why explore these more challenging aspects of ourselves?" Much of the new spiritual principles over the last twenty years has focused on affirmations, and almost exclusively on the positive. In fact, I even encourage a model I call "distracting into joy." While there is room for positive-thinking models, I have found the darker feelings are often a pathway to healing. These more challenging feelings can often lead us to much deeper aspects of ourselves. A place that feels like it is too dark to explore, may in actuality hold the key to our release.

The opportunity is to accept all aspects of ourselves. We may want to block out and cut off the bad, not wanting to look too closely, thinking, "I'm not that kind of a person." But once we get past all of that, we can embrace the fact that we have moments of hate and of violence, and even feelings of being like prisoners. We might be purposefully disconnected from this very important part of ourselves when in fact, if we explore it, acknowledge it, and release it, we may have more compassion for ourselves and for those same aspects in others. Accepting all of what we are and who we are, and not making anything right or wrong is a huge opportunity.

If you look at anger for example, if someone close to you upsets you, the anger that is unleashed can feel familiar, like a switch that gets turned on when the right trigger is present. Wouldn't it be nice to turn that automatic reactionary switch into a dimmer? With a dimmer switch you now command a rash, heated reaction to perform more like a slower, level-headed, thoughtful response. That upset, and the resulting emotions you are experiencing may actually lead you back to a time in your life when the original trauma got caught in your being; the cells may remember even though you have forgotten. The body is a miracle. It is able to retain an emotion that would otherwise stop us from continuing to live, and hold it until we are ready to release it.

Life's challenges show up, and we have a chance to explore the triggered emotions of anger, hate, jealousy, etc., then journey to those hidden places within. There, we can acknowledge the darker emotions, ask into them, determine if the beliefs held there are really true, and then duly release them. If we force ourselves to ignore these darker aspects, we are negating the elements of ourselves that require further exploration that could result in a deepening beyond our imagination.

So my suggestion is to discover and embrace your darker emotions, follow them and see where they lead. You will be amazed to see the false beliefs revealed to you through this journey, ones you may have held onto for a very long time.

Now an episode of anger becomes a key to revelation and realignment, ultimately leading to more peace, more joy, more flexibility and fewer automatic triggers into these so-called negative emotions.

"You can't have a light without a dark to stick it in." - Arlo Guthrie

You are the light
You are the dark
You are a challenge
You are an invitation
You are knowledge
You are ignorance
You are discourse
You are dialogue
You are protest
You are praise

Photo by: João Paglione

Life is Grey and It's Good

Wouldn't it be nice if life were black and white? The answers would either be right or wrong. It would be utterly clear what was good or bad. We live in a world where free will and choice create many layers of grey. We experience a life that offers a unique proving ground where the truth is different for each of us. I remember hearing once that the Golden Rule in the wrong hands might not be so great. In the extreme, for example, if a sadomasochist does unto others as he would have done unto him, it might not be too pleasant for the "others" who are not sadomasochists.

Interacting with and being in relationship with another being is one big huge mass of grey. Each of us brings our individual ancestry, family background, culture (and for those of you who believe in reincarnation, past lives) to each relationship, and, as a result, the level of potential confusion that can occur is quite amazing. What is even more amazing is that we can get along at all, and that we can communicate as well as we do. It is a true testament to human nature that we have been able to survive so long and have, so many times in history and probably in our own lives, found our way through horrible circumstances through communication with others and with ourselves.

So what is right? What is wrong? What do you believe right now? Do you believe you live in an abundant and joyful universe? Do you believe life is a bitch and then you die? Do you believe that life is a series of tests, like a classroom? Do you believe that you have no control over your life? Do you believe that life happens for a reason and it is your job to determine that reason?

Whatever you believe is the truth for you, and the universe will support you in that belief. There is no wrong, there is just what is. The evidence of your life influences what you believe to be true about your life. So if the evidence of your life is that it is hard and that "they" are out to get you, then that is what your life will be.

So what if you decide you are going to create new evidence for a different kind of life? What if you decide that you live in a universe that is safe, easy and effortless? Then that will be the truth for you, and the universe will now support you in that truth by providing those experiences. The challenge is that we have these habits, these ways of thinking about our lives, that are sometimes difficult to let go of. The evidence of the old life is clear, and just stating that we have this new life may seem hard, at first, to stick with. Simply declaring "I live in a universe that is safe, easy and effortless" isn't going to wipe the slate clean, or is it?

"In the right light, at the right time, everything is extraordinary." - Aaron Rose

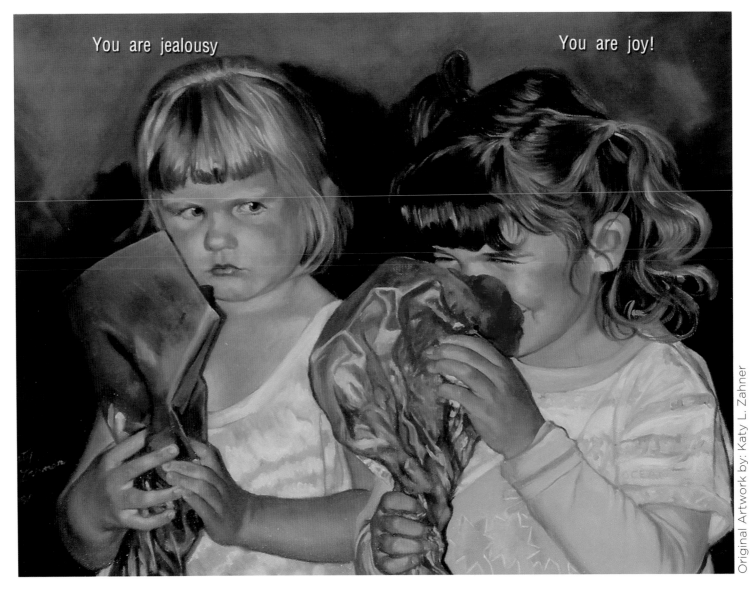

You are jealousy

You are joy!

With each EMOTION expressed comes UNDERSTANDING, and with understanding comes the opportunity for FORGIVENESS.

Original Artwork by: Katy L. Zahner

Jealousy or Love?

Jealousy is a condition, and love is a way of being. That being said, they are both reflections of the inner dialogue within you. Just look at these little girls. They both received the same gift of a flower, but one chooses to see it as glorious and the other chooses to view the joy of her sister as competition, perhaps coming from a place of lack, the sense of "I don't have enough," or "I'm missing something that someone else has." Lack is a man-made creation, and jealousy is generally an emotion that comes from believing in the illusion of lack. There really is no lack in the world; there is enough of everything for everyone, always.

The truth of this is found in the Law of Attraction, which is how energy works in the universe, whereby your thoughts create your reality. If you see and feel only lack, then the universe will agree with you and lack will appear as true for you. If you believe in love, goodness and plenty, that will be your experience. Whenever we have faced a time of "there is no way this will ever happen," it has happened because someone believed it was possible: electricity, breaking the sound barrier, going to the moon all seemingly impossible, yet all a reflection of abundance in thought and creativity.

Back to jealousy, any emotion can be a teacher, and if we look at jealousy it is also a valuable teacher. Any thoughts within us, whether they are dark thoughts or lighter thoughts, are a means to an end, and a catalyst for change. We may be jealous of someone, yet discover that that person actually has his or her own life challenges that we can really identify with. Or perhaps the individual worked extremely hard to achieve success, and that person's work ethic and determination can serve as an inspiration. At that moment of realization, jealousy can quickly turn to respect.

The universe provides us with just such an emotion in order to allow us to be humbled by it and then have the potential to grow beyond its pettiness. It also shows us a new path to our own success, such as, "if they can do it, then so can I!" This realization is a reflection of natural flow occurring. Again, the jealousy that is within us is ready to be released.

"Happiness cannot be traveled to, owned, earned, worn or consumed. Happiness is the spiritual experience of living every minute with love, grace and gratitude." – Denis Waitley

You are success

You are ecstasy

You are gratitude

You are desolation

You are bliss

You are failure

You are abundance

You are rapture

You are delight

You are misery

You are debt

You are grief

You are poverty

You are money

You are pleasure

You are agony

Photo by: Jennifer McLean

Exploring the Body

Success/failure, poverty/abundance–there is a razor's edge between these dualities. In each moment we are seconds away from pleasure or agony. How do you cope with these experiences?

As a healer, one thing I have noticed in working with so many souls (and their bodies) is that the body encapsulates every emotion and each of these dualities. My specialization is healing trauma. I see trauma at the foundation of every symptom and disease. At the core of the trauma is a thought. It was the thought that occurred at the moment of the traumatic event that got locked into the body's tissue.

The trauma is now an irritation and creates an energy block. Like a boulder that falls into a river the qui / energy stream of the body has to find its way around this obstacle. This shows up as psychological workarounds (denial, procrastination, self-sabotage) and, in most instances, eventually shows up as pain and physical dis-ease. The purpose of our life is to explore the shadow, the darker emotions, for it is in those dark places where the light can shine brightest. Exploring all your feelings allows for release of old irrelevant trauma and the opening for new levels of lightness, ease and grace.

The body is the best place to explore to find if you are holding back flow in your life. It can serve as the most important barometer of health and happiness. By checking in with your body, going inside and simply observing energy, sensation and feeling states, you can find those lost moments of trauma that are causing you to work around your own energy. Then you can clear them to lighten your spiritual (and physical) load.

In quantum physics, "the observer effect" refers to changes that the act of observing will make on the phenomenon being observed. In the healing process, this translates to observing, or appreciating your energetic system as it expresses itself. As you watch the energetic movement of the blocks and releases, the body knows that you are paying attention and alters and reorganizes into a new system or pattern of renewed health and balance. Within these patterns are the old feelings and beliefs that, once acknowledged, can change into newfound harmony.

The safest place on the planet is always in your own body. Many of us souls, through trauma or even spiritual practices, have left our bodies to one degree or another. Go inside whenever you can, explore what is there. It offers the gift of memories and spiritual exploration resulting in clearing the old debris and re-patterning into more openness, intimacy and flow. When you are in flow, what I call "the zone," you can actually feel all the possibilities that are available to you. The time is now... go inside and take a look.

"Good for the body is the work of the body, good for the soul the work of the soul, and good for either the work of the other." – Henry David Thoreau

You are closed

You are discriminating

You are unreasonable

You are unprovoked

You are fair

You are mean

You are gossip

You are equitable

You are commonsensical

You are reasonable

You are shrewd

You
are
o
p
e
n

You are bad-tempered

You are irrational

You are practical

Don't Complain and Don't Explain

My grandmother often said, "Don't complain and don't explain." It is something that comes to mind whenever I catch myself whining or gossiping about someone else, or justifying something I am doing, or trying to find "allies" who will back up my negative world view or opinion. Gossip is one of the most dangerous activities and also one of the most enticing. Gossip is where ugly rumors start that contribute to the most hurtful kind of dysfunction. In the business world it is called triangulation, meaning talking about a third party with someone else instead of directly confronting the source of the problem. Nothing gets accomplished by talking around the person or talking about the person behind his or her back. That is not to say that it is always in your best interest to "confront"; in many cases this would be foolhardy. However, spinning your wheels in the rut of gossip and complaining does you far more harm than good. It taints the well of good intentions and damages reputations and perceptions, especially your own.

Many times challenging situations in which we feel compelled to gossip are actually opportunities–invitations to change how we see ourselves through the eyes of others. Remember the idea of "you are all that is?" It means, that person is also a reflection of you.

So look again and gauge whether what you are seeing / what they are projecting is the truth of who you are or not. The need for gossip disappears when you can look at the person from the perspective of "is what they are doing / what I am judging / what I am gossiping about a reflection of some aspect of me?" Then the opportunity is there to look inside and see what they are reflecting back to you. The person you are judging is reflecting a truth about yourself that you are ready to look at and release.

You have life challenges because you are ready for them!

Think about the things that you perceive to be "happening to you." Nothing happens to you; it happens as a result of your belief systems.

So, it appears that you have it all together; you are a good person and it may seem like you don't deserve this "thing" that happened to you. However, there are deep-seated beliefs that have gotten stuck in your subconscious and cellular memory that are causing those beliefs to manifest themselves in the world.

If there is still violence in the world then there is still violence in each of us.

If there is still hunger in the world then there is still a sense of lack within us.

If there is still illness and disease in the world then there is still illness and disease in us.

If there is still hunger in the world then there is still a sense of lack within us.

You Are

The wind in the trees
The trickling of the stream
The roar of the white water
The whoosh of the waterfall
The sound of rain
The booming of thunder
The crashing of the waves
The bark of a dog
The meow of a cat
The cry of a baby
Laughing
Music
The flush of a toilet
The crackling of frying bacon
The bubbling of cooking soup
The murmur of prayer

Photo by: Jennifer McLean

We are all part of the "all that is," and therefore, if anything going on in your surroundings feels "off," then something in you is off. This external "offness" is just a prompt, a catalyst for you to take a closer look. It is the miracle of noticing, and recognizing yourself in everything, that can turn life's challenges into life's opportunities.

The things that are coming at you are life experiences you have created because you are ready to release the old junk. Isn't this a much more helpful way to look at the perceived challenges of your life? You are ready for the next iteration of yourself, and in order for that next best version of you to manifest itself, you must release the old energy blocks that are no longer needed.

You are no longer a victim. You created these things because you are strong enough to handle them and at a place that will let you face them, look at them, respond to them and ultimately, release them in gratitude.

When you ask for a new, bigger vision of yourself, then everything that is not in alignment with that new vision will come up to be looked at, investigated and released. You can't take this current version of you with you to the next expanded level. If you could, you would already be in the full manifestation of that vision. If you aren't there yet, that means there is more to clear and let go of. No failures, no wrong, just release–always release, all the time releasing.

This is where people get stuck: they visualize it, they feel it, they sense it, and then when the old junk comes up for viewing and release they think, "This isn't working." Well, everything is working perfectly, and the old is coming up because you asked for the universe to reveal what might be in your way, and, most importantly, because you are at a place in your life where you have the tools and strength of character to face these demons once and for all.

It All Comes Back to What You Believe

If you believe that you can declare it and it is so, then it is. But we have these minds that question and probe and have to see something to believe it. We have these neural pathways that have established roadways (or ruts) of thinking. No matter, it all comes down to simply believing it and confirming it true in your experience. That new belief will form new neural pathways and that truth will now be your life.

What does "simply believe it" mean? You have to feel to the depth of your being that this new life is the truth of you. You have to see it in your mind's eye, feel it, taste it, smell it, hear it. Experience all the senses and explore the vision of this new life. Then, most importantly, you have to feel it emotionally. As you envision this new life you must sense the emotions of that life. When you see yourself in a new job, new car, new relationship, new house, whatever, feel the joy of it, feel the fun in it, experience the laughter in it. Feel true happiness.

If there is still violence in the world then there is still violence in each of us.

You are Peace   You are forgiveness   You are Care   You are Depression

You are Youth

You are OLD AGE

You are Winning

You are Losing

You are Joy

You are wrinkle

You are a smile

You are contentment   You are a grimace   You are plastic surgery

YOU ARE TOUGHNESS   You are Serenity   You are Hate

The study of the brain has established that the brain can find ways of adapting, and we can use this capability to create completely new lives for ourselves.

Let's say you decide that you now live in an abundant, safe and joyful universe; that everything in your life will, from now on, reflect that abundance, safety and joy. There are several things that will likely happen: First, evidence of the previous belief system will still probably appear here and there to give you the opportunity to let it go (but only if you believe that). Second, evidence of the new belief system will also appear. This is a key part of the process–how you respond to these forms of evidence. Do you look at the old negative stuff that is showing up and say to yourself, "See, this is proof, I can't do this," and then stop working toward your dream? Or do you look at it as an opportunity to affirm your new life? You have the choice to look at

this old stuff and change it. What better way to affirm the new life than to use the old as a point of reference, something that contrasts your new vision with the old? Then make adjustments accordingly!

For example, let's say you are a salesperson and seem to constantly attract mean clients, or control freaks who lack integrity. You have decided that you are now attracting clients who are supportive, respectful and honest. So, when the next client is a mean control freak and lies, here is your chance to see what your thoughts previously made manifest, then use that result to draw a distinction between the two, and say a stronger yes again to the new (and no to the old).

What Does this Transformation Look Like?

First, take yourself out of the feeling of "Ugh, this will never change"

to a new place of "Hmmm, this is interesting." From here you can review the situation and reflect again on your vision: "I now have an even clearer picture of the new truth, that I work with supportive, respectful and honest clients." I am sure you can come up with a million reasons why this won't work: "My boss won't let me drop this client," "I need the money and have to put up with it," "There are no good clients," and on and on. But, you see, these words are the same old negative affirmations telling the universe that these beliefs are the truth for you, and as result they will simply self-perpetuate.

Instead, take a step back, stop reacting and start responding. See these clients for who they are: flawed beings just trying to get by. This is the way they learned to behave. It is not up to you to teach these individuals a lesson or change them; it is up to you to accept the situation and be as kind and giving as you can.

If there is still illness and disease in the world
then there is still illness and disease in us.

YOU are the OCEAN

Photo by: Jennifer McLean

you are the ea r th

you are the sky

you are a n atom

you are a nu c leus

you are the at o m bomb

you are h e alth

you are si c kness

you are sci e nce fiction

you are a good novel

you are a cting

you are m u sic

you are rh y thm

you are the cure for cancer

Take the high road and don't buy into the image they are portraying. Then use a flawed client as a foil to imagine the opposite. List all the things that are opposite to that client. List the things that you would want in a "perfect" client. If you didn't have this supposedly rotten client to show you what you don't want, then it would be harder to figure out what you do want. Then visualize and experience the new client with all your five senses. Use your emotions to feel the joy, exhilaration and enthusiasm you experience when you are with that new client.

There is another important area to explore here: what is the challenging client reflecting back to you? In fact, in any area of your life, when someone shows up that is pushing your buttons they are there because they reflect that aspect inside of you that you are ready to release. Everyone you interact with is an aspect of you. The person that may have wronged you is actually an aspect of you trying to get your attention. The easiest route

for most of us is to blame that person for their behavior, shake our head and say, "how could they?" Instead we can stop and review within ourselves, "When have I exhibited that behavior in the past?" "When have I ever been mean or unkind or petulant?" etc. And that includes deeds, words and thoughts. Then the opportunity is to forgive yourself and release that old belief and feel differently about yourself. Feeling differently will change the situation.

One of the key actions is to also feel the feelings of what you want. The challenge is knowing how to feel something that you have never experienced before. The starting point is to use your imagination to envision what it might feel like, and then go from there. You will be given an experience that allows you to have a sense for what it feels like. This is like physical training–you have to strengthen that "feeling" muscle.

Each time you are given an opportunity, feel what the end result

is, even if it is just for a second. For example, I cashed a check at one bank so my bank wouldn't hold the funds. I had a couple thousand dollars in my pocket. This money was pretty much already spent on bills and such, but it felt really good to have a couple thousand dollars in my pocket for a few minutes. I paused for a second and really felt what this wealth felt like, exercising the "wealth feeling" muscle. Now I can access that muscle more readily because I felt it once. The key was that I acknowledged this new feeling in the moment and took pains to remember it for use in my visioning.

What does it feel like in your body when you are doing what you love? Grow that feeling muscle so that each time you feel it you know you are on the right path. What fills you up? What drives your passion? If you had a magic wand and could sweep it over your life, what would you ideally be doing and, more importantly, what would it feel like?

What does it feel like in your body when you are doing what you love?

The Pitcher

If we don't take care of **ourselves** there isn't enough left over to share with others think of it like a pitcher...the pitcher needs to be refilled.if it doesn't get refilled regularly, there is nothing left to offer; it **dries** up. MAKE sure you take time to fill your **Pitcher** then pour away and **Share** the **BEST OF YOU**

Photo by: Richard Wanderman

Let's revisit the client example. Here is what will happen by envisioning a better outcome: the challenging client will either go away (transfer or quit) or will transform before your very eyes, or you will get another job that is compatible with this new truth that you envisioned. But the "how" of it doesn't matter; it is the "what" and the trust and faith in the manifestation that matters.

Just like anything, this takes dedication and commitment. You have to believe 100% in this new truth and this new life you are creating. You have to see it and emotionally feel it. You have to trust that when old stuff comes knocking you can say, "Thanks for the reminder." It is there to prompt you about what you are now creating that is different from it and what you are ready to explore deeper, forgive and release.

As mentioned earlier, this process also includes looking within at what this client is reflecting back to you *about* you. Think of something this client "did to you." Now take a look within yourself. Has there ever been a time in your life when you have done something similar to someone else or yourself? Where you have done some damage to another in a moment of emotional reaction?

Well then, this person is the gift that you have created to show you what you are ready to release. This person and his or her actions directly reflect actions you have taken in the past. That is why they are here now. These life situations show up over and over again.

This is life, this is the journey, to reflect in the moment on our feelings, forgiving ourselves for having them, and being grateful for what they are

here to show us. This isn't a one time "phew, glad that's over" thing. It is an interactive, iterative process that continues our whole lives.

You say to yourself, "Yeah, but I don't do that anymore." Well, the memories are still held in your body. The guilt is still held in memory. The opportunity is to forgive yourself for those past actions that are energetically similar to what is now being "perpetrated" on you.

Go inside yourself. Dialogue with this aspect of your past actions held in cellular memory, ask that aspect of yourself what it needs, forgive yourself, feel the feelings of forgiveness and love, and release it.

"You see things and you say, Why?
But I dream things that never were and say, Why not?"
- George Bernard Shaw

Exercise: Releasing Emotions

Go inside your body. Start by taking several deep breaths (10 seconds in and 10 seconds out). Imagine that your consciousness is like a beautiful perfect pearl and it is dropped into the pool of your being. This pearl floats down into your body until it finds a place of rest, which is the center of your being. As it floats down, you feel more and more relaxed.

Once you are in your place of center, pretend you can open your eyes inside your body. Now take a look around and see if you can identify the places in your body where there is emotional tension. Find the one that is calling you the most, the place that says, "Come here first." Go to that place in your body and ask it, "How have you served me?" and/or "What are you doing here?" The opportunity is to explore the thought behind the emotions, the original emotional trauma that found a home in your body and that continues to impact how you behave in certain situations.

Have a conversation with this aspect of yourself and allow yourself to be open to whatever comes forth. It might be an incident or simply the raw emotion finally being exposed and ready for release. Simply feeling the emotion might be all you need to do. Don't let the emotion take over. No more than a minute or so of the feeling is good...this is a release, not an indulgence of the feeling. If you are starting to feel overwhelmed by the feeling, just take a long deep breath; your breath dissipates emotions. Take a couple of these breaths until you find equilibrium again.

Photo by: Alexander Gobell

Forgiveness: Taking Care of Yourself

The synonyms for forgiveness include "pardon," "clemency," "absolution," "mercy," "amnesty," and "exoneration." Interestingly, many of these words seem to let the person you are forgiving off the hook, so to speak. In fact, what forgiveness really does is get you off the hook of anxiety, anger, personality disorders, chaos and so on.

"Forgiveness" is a loaded word. From my experience it is virtually impossible to just forgive. Forgiveness is a distinct process. And I have learned that the process is not necessarily one that we would think might lead to forgiveness. The process is one of actually taking care of ourselves, no matter what.

It is important for us to take care of ourselves, especially with regard to our need for safety and protection, because it is usually our sense of safety that was betrayed in the first place; feeling a sense of betrayal or hurt created the need for forgiveness.

It is when we take care of ourselves that we can clearly see who the perpetrators really are or were, and how we are no longer affected by them. Then we can truly, profoundly forgive. But how do you forgive the unforgivable? This process is further clarified in the story below.

For most, it probably won't be having "them" say, "I'm sorry," or even hearing yourself say, "I forgive you." Those are just words. The true goal is to find peace of mind and a sense of fullness, recapturing a piece of yourself that may have been lost many years ago. Forgiveness starts with a commitment to being the best person you can be. This doesn't mean being "good"; it means being true to you. In a way it is almost being self-centered, in that you are focused on what it will take for you to feel the safest in any given situation. I don't mean "safe" in the sense of not leaving the house or doing things differently from your normal routine, but managing to be in and of the world in a way that suits you. Forgiveness doesn't mean you have to hang out with the people you are forgiving, or even talk to them again, for that matter. It means doing for you what makes you feel balanced and grounded and secure as you go out and live your life.

There is a path to forgiveness. You cannot simply say, "I forgive you" unless you feel it. Those words mean nothing if you still have that deep-seated resentment simmering inside. Forgiveness means seeing those who have hurt you in a new light. It can come from knowing that soul part of you that has never been hurt or harmed and can never be anything less than all-that-is. The result of forgiveness is feeling safe and good about yourself. From it comes the natural feeling of affection and love.

"You are exactly who you need to be in this moment. Don't begrudge that or justify it."- Jennifer McLean

TRUTH creates *change*

The fact that fiber is an important word in our dietary vocabulary is an example of positive change. For many years I was troubled by the large multinational packaged goods companies that had a huge amount of control over what we ate. Their focus and attention was on their shareholders and profits and not on how additives and lack of fiber in our food, not to mention the large volume of sodium and sugar, were contributing to a growing nutritional health crisis. But the truth about nutrition has seeped out, and even these companies are being forced to change. The fact that one of the best-known white bread brands on the market is now including (or should I say "putting back") whole wheat in its breads illustrates the power of the truth. Each of us can make demands that can contribute to changing "the system."

Photo by: James Chiou

Forgiveness in Spite of Yourself: A Story

A woman who grew up in an alcoholic family set out on a journey of healing, starting an ongoing process of getting to know herself and understanding what she liked, wanted and rejected. She experimented with many different modalities of healing, from the extremes of alternative "woo woo" to more practical psychiatry, even pharmaceuticals. Over the years she arrived at a simple truth: communicate, ask for what you need and take care of yourself. Through many life and relationship experiences she discovered elements of this truth. One in particular occurred through the process of addressing her father's drinking problem.

She had reached a point where she could no longer be present when her father drank. She told her father that when he drank in front of her she would leave. He was a longtime alcoholic, and one day prior to a family gathering she had a conversation with him, probably one of the first real conversations of their relationship. She didn't ask him to stop drinking; she just told him that she wouldn't remain to witness it. The key is that she took the first steps to really taking care of herself.

Instead of putting up with the uncomfortable conduct of her drunken father at gatherings and family outings, she left. As soon as he took his first drink, she left, not with a big huffy farewell, just a simple good-bye. She didn't lie and say she had another engagement; she just left. When people would ask her why she was leaving, she would say, "It is time for me to go."

An interesting thing happens when you modify your behavior: others' actions escalate. They turn up the volume and increase the pressure on you to continue to "play," to play the role that everyone had agreed upon and had been participating in for years. That role for her had been one of being the "mouth," the one who got openly upset when her father drank and made snide comments to others about it. She always stayed to witness just how awful it was going to get so she could comment on it afterward. This new code of conduct–her choosing leaving– was a significant turn of events. She said she was going to leave; she even told her father it was to "take care of herself," because when he drank it brought up bad memories she no longer wished to experience. Bottom line: when he drank she left.

The final event that challenged her, and in turn changed this particular pattern for good, occurred a couple of years later. Her mother and father were in a hotel near where she lived. She was visiting them in their room when her father had his first drink, once again testing her resolve, seeing if she would play her old role again. This was the first time in a long time that the daughter didn't just leave immediately.

"Life is a juicy adventure of wonderful experiences deepening our expression of the divine." - Jennifer McLean

Photo by: Jennifer McLean

You are
You are Islam
Christianity You are the Kabbalah
You are You are Jesus
Buddha You are Judaism
You are Buddhism You are You
you are joel osteen Billy Graham are the
Rev. Michael Torah
Beckwith You are Faith
You are
your. neighbor You are You are me

They went to dinner and the father kept leaving to sneak a drink, each time coming back drunker. At one point the mother turned to her and asked her, "What do you want?" referring to the menu. She turned to her mother and said quietly, "What do I want? I want to go home." She got up from the table and left. Her father was just coming back from the room after having another "nip"; he caught her at the door and asked where she was going. She told him she was going home. He was very upset that she was leaving, not angry but hurt.

He asked why, and she told him the truth: "I can't be with you when you drink. It is upsetting, and I must leave." He never drank in front of her again.

What happened for him to change his behavior? She didn't ask him to stop. She simply took care of herself. It was his choice to not drink in her presence. To further qualify this: it was never her goal for him to stop drinking. By taking care of herself and having only that as her intention, and without trying to control anyone else, she ultimately accomplished much more– she started healing her relationship with her father.

Taking care of herself started the path to forgiveness. This was not an intentional act but something that simply happened and surprised her more than anything she could have imagined. After she stumbled onto this approach with this experience, she started seeing the pattern in it and applied it with more intention in her daily life. But what she didn't realize at the time was that this pattern had a name. It was forgiveness.

She accepted her father and his drinking, assuming that it would not change. She took care of herself, and in the process, she realized, in hindsight, she forgave him.

This snuck up on her. It was not something she was looking for or even asked for. It just happened. But why? Because she was herself, comfortable in the knowledge that she was consistently making choices that would allow her to feel safe with her father. Now she saw him as a quirky, flawed person, like those found in all corners of the world, someone just trying to get by. She accepted him for who he was and appreciated herself in that process.

She suddenly, in a moment, realized the miracle of what forgiveness meant–feeling safe and good about herself, feeling affection and love, seeing those who had hurt her in a new light.

In this moment she did in fact experience the dictionary definition: "pardon," "clemency" and "absolution." However, she was the one who was pardoned. She was absolved of her own pain and found clemency for herself in her life. And she never once needed to utter the words, "You're forgiven."

"A mind stretched to a new idea never
goes back to its original form."
-Oliver Wendell Holmes

Ho'oponopono Prayer

I'm Sorry

Please Forgive Me

I Love You

Thank You

Is it Injustice or Life?

"It's not fair. It just doesn't seem right. The injustice of it. I can't believe that something like this could happen." Boy, these are thoughts that have plagued me in my life. As I've matured I have often experienced moments of seeming injustice that in hindsight turned out to be exactly right. I have also witnessed that old adage, "What goes around comes around."

There was a woman who was an extreme narcissist, and I had a tediously difficult time navigating her narcissistic world view. Essentially, through sheer force of will and breaking people down, she got her way over and over again. Those who were directly impacted by her manipulation and backstabbing always had an extreme sense of the injustice of it. That someone so deceitful and uncaring of others would consistently "get her way" was frustrating.

I reflected back on a series of traumatic situations she had created, and even though it appeared that she had gotten her way, she never found happiness in those moments. She just moved from one crisis to the next, in a series of events that created a very unhappy life.

In my most extreme moments of being affected by her, I still had a happier life and could walk away intact in my own being from the onslaught of crises she created. The appearance of unfairness was just that, an appearance. In fact, she continues to have an unjust life.

Essentially, there really is no "fair." There is no "equitable." There just is what is. That doesn't mean you don't have reactions and feelings toward "injustice." That is the purpose of these events, to trigger something inside you to assist you in changing your thoughts, which in turn will change your life.

Now on a world scale, injustice is a very real occurrence and certainly seems to be more difficult to position as "It's all you." Those still in prison camps who have no recourse, the slaughters in Rwanda, the mistreatment of women in Afghanistan. How could these things happen?

I still believe that there is a divine order in everything, even in these happenings. That is not to say that you sit back and say, "Oh well, they created it. They chose this." No!

These events and these injustices are an opportunity to look at what's been created in the world; they are a catalyst for each of us to take a stand and do something. When we as individuals move into the world and out of our safe soccer-mom, get-a-paycheck existence and start giving back, and make a contribution in some new meaningful way we can actually change the world!

"Happiness is a butterfly, which when pursued, is always just beyond your grasp, but which, if you will sit down quietly, may alight upon you"
- Nathaniel Hawthorne

Original Artwork by: Michael Ringer
Song Lyrics by: Keith and Maura Leon

I AM THE LIGHT (a song)

I am the light,

I am the Love,

I am the Spirit, ME

I am the Peace,

that's healing the world,

I am the answer, ME

I am the answer, ME

I am the answer, ME

owever, to change the macro events we have to start micro. We start with ourselves.

How do we free the prisoners of the world? Free ourselves. How do we stop suffering? Look around at your friends and family, at the members of your community, and lend a hand to stop their suffering. Offer your God-given talents and time and make a difference. There is a plan for you. Go into the world and find out what it is. Do you want abundance? Help someone else achieve it. Do you want a house? Help someone build his or her house.

Do you want a healthy relationship? Love yourself, then work at a battered women's shelter and help the women get back on their feet, showing them by example that loving themselves will bring healthy relationships. Do you want more spirituality in your life? Volunteer at your church or spiritual center.

Giving is a key part of receiving.

Giving will contribute to the reduction of injustice in the world. Look around. What can you give back?

If you simply can't volunteer then take the time to appreciate someone else's dream. Acknowledge their vision, share how you want to be their first customer. "Wow" their plans. Make an effort to support another's contribution. You will be enriched by this experience as well.

Many of us are paralyzed by the depth and breadth of changes that need to occur in the world. How can we as individuals possibly make a difference? You can change your thoughts. You can create an internal sense of peace that creates a wave of peace on the planet.

I had a powerful vision about this. I was exploring my own internal violence while driving one day and something happened:

I had just turned a corner, and a man riding a bike fell right there on the sidewalk as I witnessed it. He didn't fall horribly. He got up a little shaken and brushed himself off and rode away, but it was sudden and shocking, as those things are. I was curious as to why I witnessed that. While I don't think I "made" him fall, I do understand now that we co-created the moment. I wanted to explore this further, so I pulled the car over. I took a moment and looked inside, and what that moment triggered was a sense of violence. What I saw was the part of my unconscious limbic brain that somehow appreciated violence. As I looked deeper, I witnessed the larger-scale violence in the world and then saw that same energy of violence in me. I felt at a deep level the oneness with this group agreement regarding violence, and again saw it in myself and felt a sense that we are all one, in our inner-peace and our inner-violence.

I believe that we are all connected, kind of like the Pando (Trembling Giant) quaking aspen grove in Utah, which is actually one huge tree that is part of a system of "treeness," all connected by one set of roots.

"Far away there in the sunshine are my highest aspirations. I may not reach them, but I can look upon and see their beauty, believe in them and try to follow where they lead." - Louisa May Alcott

You are the Stars

You are the

You are the UNIVERSE

You are the galaxy You are You the cell You are birth You are the Milky Way

You are tsunami You are Gaia You are healing

You are bacteria You are global warming

You are an earthquake You are the planets You are the amoeba

In that moment, I had a vision:

I saw that because I am part of everything I have a hand in creating all of it, including violence. What comes into my radar or within my purview is a personal creation. As I look within I can really see the energy that I commit to creating everything in my life. I can see the strings of attachment that project out from me, making things, thoughts and beliefs real.

As I explored within myself how I felt about violence and wars and crime, I saw the strings of my personal deep-seated unconscious beliefs move into the world and attach to violent "things" and events. I then saw thousands of other strings attached from other minds, which in aggregate made the picture whole (a hologram), like a Seurat painting in which all the individual dots together form a picture.

Every day since that first exploration of violence, when I have a moment of frustration or an angry outburst, I immediately do my inner work and recognize the violence that is within me. I see how my emotions and infrastructure of beliefs can show up in the world and result in that creep cutting me off, or that person at the grocery store being unpleasant, or even the war.

As I acknowledge and recognize these strings of belief manifesting and creating my reality, and shift those feelings, changing my mind, I witness my belief string disengaging. When I observe this internal vision of my personal belief string releasing, I also notice that others are disrupted into disengagement. Like a pyramid of apples, if you remove one from the middle, the rest either settle into a new configuration or fall.

The Theory of the 100th Monkey

The Japanese monkey, Macaca fuscata, had been observed in the wild for a period of over 30 years.

In 1952, on the island of Koshima, scientists were providing monkeys with sweet potatoes dropped in the sand. The monkeys liked the taste of the raw sweet potatoes, but they found the dirt unpleasant.

An 18-month-old female named Imo found she could solve the problem by washing the potatoes in a nearby stream. She taught this trick to her mother. Her playmates also learned this new way and they taught their mothers too.

This cultural innovation was gradually picked up by various monkeys before the eyes of the scientists. Between 1952 and 1958 all the young monkeys learned to wash the sandy sweet potatoes to make them more palatable. Only the adults who imitated their children learned this social improvement. Other adults kept eating dirty sweet potatoes.

Then something startling took place. In the autumn of 1958, a certain number of Koshima monkeys were washing sweet potatoes – the exact number is not know. (continues on next page »)

You
are life

You are waiting   You are walking

You are running   You are crying   You are laughing

You are singing You are enjoying You are pain You are disease

You are wisdom   You are immaturity   You are right   You are wrong You are death

You are alive

If my postulation of "we are all one" is true, then if my string of belief disengages, it causes a ripple effect on the whole. My release of my feelings and beliefs relating to violence allows an easing of the tension of the whole.

That is the 100th monkey theory and Carl Jung's "collective unconsciousness" theory in action. Our own internal work resolving our part in the resonant global beliefs and extreme emotional energies can change the whole. Each of us plays a part, and the more we take personal responsibility for our internal beliefs and feelings, then change them, the greater the opportunity for achieving critical mass and sudden shifts into peace. The cautionary tale is: that same critical mass is also applicable to war.

YOU, right now as the single entity you are, can change the whole by adopting a new intention for peace; pausing in the middle of an argument and seeing the other person's perspective; or, by releasing your own internal derisiveness and forgiving yourself. Your individual shifts can be the catalyst for world peace.

March 7, 1944:
"I lie in bed at night, after ending my prayers
with the words,'thank you God for all that
is good and dear and beautiful,'
and I'm filled with joy...At such moments
I don't think about all the misery,
but about the beauty that still remains..."

Anne Frank from *The Diary of Anne Frank*

Let us suppose that when the sun rose one morning there were 99 monkeys on Koshima Island who had learned to wash their sweet potatoes. Let's further supposed that later that morning, the hundredth monkey learned to wash potatoes.

But notice: A surprising thing observed by these scientists was that the habit of washing sweet potatoes then jumped over the sea... Colonies of monkeys on other islands and the mainland troop of monkeys at Takasakiyama began washing their sweet potatoes.

Thus, when a certain critical number achieves an awareness, this new awareness may be communicated from mind to mind.

Although the exact number may vary, this Hundredth Monkey Phenomenon means that when only a limited number of people know of a new way, it may remain the conscious property of these people.

But there is a point at which if only one more person tunes in to a new awareness, a field is strengthened so that this awareness is picked up by almost every one!

from the book:
The Hundredth Monkey by Ken Keys, Jr.

You are
justice

You are
injustice

You are
impunity

You are
uncertainty

You are
lust

You are
punishment

You are
trust

You are
a child

You are
a pet

You are
affection

You are
prison

You are
a prisoner

Photo by: Ruth Savitz

Releasing a Person: An Exercise

This is an energetic/meditative Body Dialog exercise that can assist you in releasing a person who you may feel is harming you, or is a potential energy vampire, or who just plain ticked you off.

Do this as many times as needed, there are layers to every relationship, and each time your do this Body Dialog you are stripping away the most current and relevant layers of dysfunction–freeing you both.

Picture the person you want to let go of standing in front of you. Imagine an absolutely stunning crystal rock the size of a large mansion. This crystal is exactly the right crystal for the person you are releasing. Inside the crystal is everything this person would ever want or dream of. His or her heart's desires are contained in this crystal rock. Picture the person going into the rock and getting to experience everything he or she ever wanted. Then step back and turn the rock so you can no longer see the person or the entrance to the rock.

Take a look at all the energetic lines that are hooking you into this person. There are huge rope-like things, small wispy tethers, sticky messy sinews, rubber band-like strings. All of these are hooked into you from this person and from you into this person.

Now, imagine you have a sword made of light and love, like a sword of magic loving energy that can only cut cords of dysfunction. Then start cutting these lines of energetic dysfunction, disengaging the attachments to this person. As you are doing this, notice if there are any that slither back to reconnect.

Do this for as long as is necessary, with strong intention of releasing these attachments. See the energy coming from above, from the source, and also feel the nourishment from below, like a tree with roots getting energy from the earth. This is where healthy energy comes from, from above and below, not from the other person.

Next, give the rock house a little push with your foot. Let the house gently, lovingly float away or slide down a hill. It might fade away until you can no longer see it, or it may just move a couple hundred yards. Take care of any energetic tethers that you may have missed. Finally, surround the distant rock (and if you can no longer see it, imagine it) with a beautiful purple flame, the purple flame of God's unconditional love. Then let it go. Feel the sense of release and relief and joy in both of you.

"Be kind and merciful. Let no one ever come to you without coming away better and happier. Be the living expression of God's kindness."
- Mother Teresa

You are the
snow

You are
technology

You are the
sky

You are the

w
a
t
e
r

You are
free

You
are
a
tree

You
are
i
n
v
e
n
t
i
v
e

You
are
a
cat

You
are
a
d
o
g

You
are
TV

You
are a *bird*

You are
a
flower

You are
grass

The "No Compromise" Theory

Okay, here is a big one for you: Don't compromise, ever. Not ever, not once, not again, ever.

You are probably thinking at this stage, "Okay, this woman is nuts." Life IS compromise, right? Relationships are compromise. It is always one big vat of compromise. Well, I am here to tell you that as soon as you compromise over anything, the next feeling is resentment. And if you feel resentment you just cut yourself off from the flow of life.

Compromise then becomes a notion of semantics. It is really a simple matter of changing your mind about something; then you are no longer compromising. So the minute it feels like you're going to have to compromise, and that sinking feeling of resentment starts to creep in, use that moment to investigate what is really going on. Go inside your body and probe into the compromise feeling to figure out what is really going on. Ask the following questions:

- What is this feeling related to in my past?

- Why am I feeling resentful?

- What is needed here for me to not feel resentful?

- How can I change my mind about this?

Here is an example of how this works:

I was coaching a husband and wife who each had diverse interests–the husband loved sports and all sporting events, and the wife loved crafts, doing them and going to craft fairs.

They each went to each other's events for a while, but the husband got to a point where he could no longer stand going to craft fairs. He had no interest in them and didn't even like the kinds of people who attended craft fairs. He was no longer willing to compromise, and we experimented with this "no compromise" theory. He decided that to release his resentment he would stop going to the craft fairs.

His wife, however, continued to attend sporting events with him. He knew his wife didn't like them and was curious about why she continued to attend, especially given his decision to stop with the craft fairs. He asked her why she continued. She answered that she saw how much he loved his sports, and it was worthwhile for her to go and experience him in his joy. She liked to watch him in his element and appreciated how happy he was and wanted to share and support him in that.

Open to a new perception of your situation
~ changing your mind changes everything.

You are valuable!

Photo by: Jennifer McLean

You are **valuable**…take that in. You are important, for real.

How does that feel inside you? Do you **believe it?** If you do, fantastic—acknowledge yourself with **large pats on the back** for seeing the value that is you.

For those of you who **still struggle** with this (even those of us who know and can usually **appreciate** our value have days and moments when that is not the case), consider this: your very **breath** is **sustaining** all the plants on the earth; they feed on CO2. So the next time you are feeling unworthy, just **take a breath.**

Well, this gave him pause, and he wondered if he could do the same.

He decided to go to the next craft fair with her with this new mindset, to support her in her joy. He went and, to his surprise, he actually had a pretty good time. He watched his wife enjoying herself, and he even witnessed how these "craft people," that he had previously dismissed, were also in their joy. He now had a better appreciation for them and he started going to the craft fairs again and having fun with his wife.

Essentially, he changed his mind about the situation, which in turn, changed his experience of the situation itself. He was able to reach a point in his thinking where going to a craft fair was no longer a compromise, but instead a joy.

The opportunity from this new perspective is to meet the moment of compromise and see if you can change your perspective. Alter your thoughts and beliefs about why you think it is a compromise. Find the moment of willingness, then do with newfound joy what just moments before had seemed like a compromise.

If you cannot find the willingness and are about to compromise yourself, simply don't do it. There will be times when compromise is a gatekeeper to keep you from doing something that is not in your highest interest. Listen to this gift of compromise, do your internal work on it, then act.

"We are not human beings on a spiritual journey.
We are spiritual beings on a human journey"
- Teilhard de Chardin

• •

"Beyond its practical aspects, gardening - be it of the soil or soul -
can lead us on a philosophical and spiritual exploration
that is nothing less than a journey into the depths of
our own sacredness and the sacredness of all beings."
- Christopher Forrest McDowell

Photo by: Jennifer McLean

You are a **sanctuary**
You are a cathedral
You are a mosque

You are a TEMPLE   You are **power**
You are worship   You are a mission

You are a synagogue   You are **community**   You are a parish

You are a synagogue   You are a tabernacle

You are a **Church**   You are family   You are a synagogue

Are You In Ego or In Love?

You have probably heard the statement that EGO means Edging God Out. I would say edging you out, but then it would be "EYO" and that isn't a word, so let's stick with God for now.

What is ego? From my perspective it is the piece of you that is hanging on to old memories, old energy blocks, the things you have not yet been able to face and release. I have even heard that it was originally designed to keep us safe and alive as we explored the higher realms of spirit. I also think it is the original brainstem responsible for flight or fight.

But then the ego got confused and thought it was in charge, and in many of us, has taken over functions not under its domain. As a result, it infuses many of the aspects of our lives with fear. Imagine a reptilian mind being in charge of how we conduct our lives.

One of the important counters to ego is love. Love allows you to be in the moment and to hear the fear but not react to it, to feel more, to negotiate life with confidence rather than defiance.

How do you know when you are working from ego or when you are working from love? Below is a chart that pretty much sums it up.

ego	love
is expectant	trusts & knows
needs	allows
seeks attention	listens
judges	forgives (through being present and in the moment)
fears	appreciates
blames	guides and acknowledges
pushes into the world	receives and embraces the world
isolates/is frenetic	is clear and smooth
is disruptive	is balanced
is disappointed	is acceptance, peace and trust

Self Portrait by: Jennifer McLean

Find your way back to love

This handy little chart on page 49, can guide you to understand when you are in ego and allow you to find its opposite - the full state of non-ego or love.

So let's say that right now you are in ego. How do you find your way back to love?

Here is a quick exercise:

Ask yourself: Is it true? Is what I am feeling, and the belief creating the feeling, true?

Then give yourself the opportunity to explore the opposite of those feelings.

Next, the opportunity is to show some gratitude, allowing this belief to seep into your consciousness, forgive yourself for having the belief, and simply love yourself for the gift that you are.

Now there is an opportunity for the ego to be in partnership with the heart, to allow the ego its domain of protection but through an understanding of the heart and love.

This creates openings instead of limitations, risking that is adventurous, not life threatening from the ego's perspective. It establishes space for both the ego *and* love, and therefore establishes balance and peace between them. This can then lead to a fulfilling life of exploration and ease.

peace

"A person never discloses his own character so clearly as when he describes another's."
- Anonymous

"All that we are is the result of what we have thought. The mind is everything. What we think, we become."
- Buddha

hope

51

"Evil" is "Live" backwards...

LIVE
EVIL

Evil is a life unlived

You are **violence**

You are **dishonor**

You are **dis**respect

You are respect

You are Love

You are be**I**ng

You are **V**alue

You are g**E**nerosity

You are support

You are elegance

you are love you are love
you are love
you are love
you are love
you are love

Evil is a Life Unlived

Years ago I was struggling with the notion of the devil. I got scared and felt like I could be attacked by the darkest of evils. I meditated on the devil and I received a vision. The vision was a sign, actually just like a street sign–on one side was "LIVE" and on the other side was "EVIL." Next, I heard, "Evil is a life unlived." That forever changed my feelings about evil.

While I do feel there is true evil in the world, the majority of evil shows up as a life unlived. The more we give in to ego, fear and hopelessness, the more an unlived life thrusts itself upon us. But please note that these feelings, in and of themselves, are not evil. They are simply lower vibrating energies showing up as negative feelings. In fact, these feelings are signposts that can be used by us to take an internal accounting of why they are here, how they have showed up and what they are showing us, that is ready to be released.

From this perspective, we now have absolute power over evil. Evil feeds on the light, but we can use the presence of evil to actually guide us deeper into the light.

The miracle of so-called negative emotions is that they can cure us of an unlived life. They can reveal to us the challenges that we are ready to let go, so we can open ourselves to the truest of lives and having a life that is fully lived.

A life that is lived is lived authentically with peace, integrity, humility, love and abundance.

I do believe there is evil in the world, but I also believe that evil cannot penetrate you unless you let it. You have to invite evil in, in order for it to influence you.

It is a simple matter of confidence and a deep faith, knowing what is right for you and what is not, and standing up for what is right. Then being in a place where your peace and love overcomes evil.

Standing up means taking stock, looking within, acknowledging, taking responsibility, releasing those things that no longer serve you, being free to live a full life.

"Whatever befalls the earth befalls the sons of the earth.
Man did not weave the web of life. He is merely a strand in it.
Whatever he does to the web, he does to himself."
- Chief Seattle

Photo by: Denzil Fernandes

You are CONNECTION

You are **bonding**

You are **friendship**

You are *acquaintance*

You are communion

You are partnership

You are acceptance

You are clashing

You are **dysfunction**

You **are** disagreement

You are arguing

You are colliding

You are harmony

You are **discord**

You are playful

The Fires of Relationship

Imagine that each individual has a fire that he or she tends to. This is the fire of the soul. Each person must take the time to nurture it, adding wood, blowing on it, keeping it going for the warmth and light it provides.

Often in relationships one of the partners leaves his or her fire to tend to the other's. If that person focuses on someone else's fire for too long, his or her own fire–the fire of the soul–eventually extinguishes. That person is missing something and can't quite put a finger on what it is. The individual has a sense that he or she has lost something in the process.

The opportunity is to always tend to your own fire of the soul within a relationship; never let your own light extinguish. Instead, both partners can take an ember from their personal fires and start a new one close by. That becomes a new entity to be nourished and loved and tended to. It takes a little more work to tend to two fires, but the warmth and light is doubled and the joint flame is a loving combination of the two souls.

There is more warmth and light in the world as a result.

"Love is like a friendship caught on fire." – Bruce Lee

The Still Point

In cranial sacral therapy, the "still point" occurs when the body goes into a state of apparent inactivity–a place of stillness.

In this stillness, however, a subtle undercurrent of true healing activity is taking place, and the opportunity for a shift into balance is available.

A "healing pulse" shows up in the still point, and often the heat of a stored energy block is released.

Emotional energies from the tissue are liberated, and the cells, muscles and surrounding area settle into a new place of being.

The body has natural healing processes that cranial sacral therapy, and other therapies, can address and stimulate. During a therapeutic healing session, there is constant changing and shifting occurring as a result. While a healing process is initiated, true resolution of an issue or

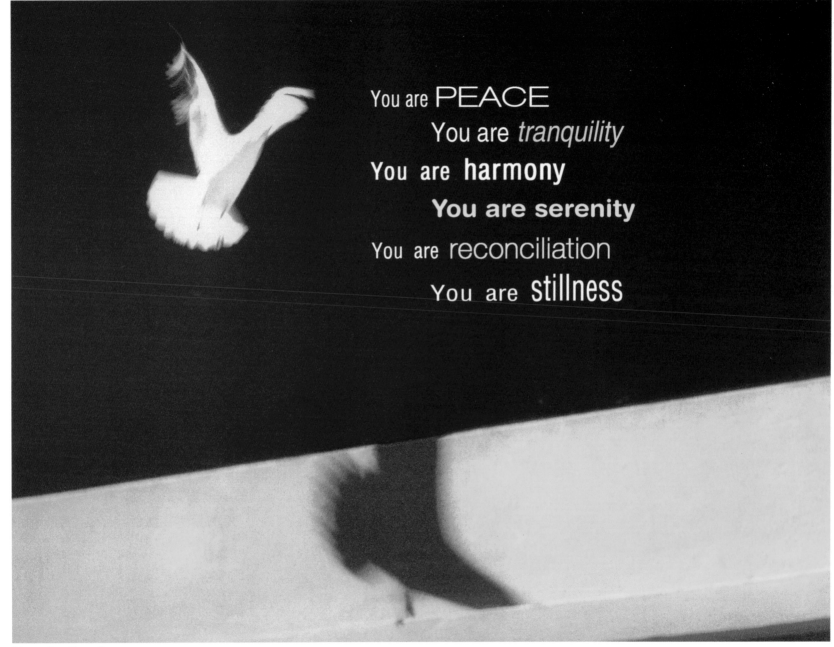

You are PEACE
You are *tranquility*
You are **harmony**
You are serenity
You are reconciliation
You are stillness

Photo by: Dan Canavan

issues occurs during a still point. The still point can happen several times during a session, or it might happen just once, but if there is a still point present, a healing resolution has generally occurred.

Still points are not just reserved for cranial sacral therapy sessions; you can also find them in nature and in your everyday life. For example, you can find still points in a river whirlpool or vortex. As the water curls around the rocks in areas of white water or eddies at the edge of the river, you will see this whirlpool effect. If you watch closely you will also see the swirl move in the opposite direction, as an antivortex. The center point between the two swirling vortexes is the point of inertia, where the movement appears to slow down.

There is a balance between the vortexes found here. The motion in opposite direction cancels out both, creating this lack of motion. This is very similar to a still point in cranial sacral therapy. When white water kayaking, this still point is where you can "surf," where you can sit in the place of inertia where the two currents cancel each other out.

When watching for vortexes in nature, see if you can find this midpoint in the currents and witness the stillness. In that moment, search for your own internal rhythm; find and match the stillness in your own being.

The still point can also apply to human activities. Within our own lives we create vortexes (and sometimes tornadoes). Within these whirlwinds of activity there are still points available to us. There is a place of calm waiting for us in every life experience.

Within those still points are found the opportunities for healing and resolution of our life issues. It is in the still place that all possibilities are available.

In the stillness you can discover a new connection to the divine or the source. This is where the wisdom shows up and reveals the nuances of change that can lead to healing.

Look around you–where are the still points in your life? What whirlwinds are you creating for yourself, and are there still points that you are overlooking?

If you can't see the stillness, go to nature and witness it there. Let it remind you and nudge you. When you find that still point in your life's activities, stay with it for a moment or two. The answers and the path to healing are waiting there for you.

"If we open a quarrel between the past and the present
we shall find that we have lost the future."
- Winston Churchill

Original Artwork by: Malcolm Brown

No is The New Yes

o makes space for yes. What you say no to can be as important as what you say yes to.

When you say no to compromise, when you say no to that moment, when you may be out of integrity, when you say no because it is time to take care of yourself, these are instances that illustrate the power of no.

I remember being in a workshop many years ago and the exercise was to say an emphatic no out loud and in a big voice. I found myself unable to do it. There was something inside of me that remembered a time in my life when saying no to someone was actually dangerous. That memory is in many of us. As children many of us were not allowed to say no.

The difference that yes can make in your life has to do with those things in your life that you are willing to take a risk for. For example, the opposite of this is not taking a risk...this may appear to be no in an instance of habit under the guise of safety (which could be a habitual mode of protection). So, you are saying no to protect yourself instead of saying no to take care of yourself, which actually pulls you out of flow. In other instances this may be saying no to what appears to be security–not wanting to "rock the boat."

An example in my own life is, I said no to corporate America, quitting my job and walking away from a paycheck after more than 20 years. Although it was scary, it opened up a whole new world and allowed me to expand my opportunities exponentially. It made room for more choices and more opportunities to express no as well as yes.

Right now in your life what would you love to say no to? What in your life is calling you to say yes. These things are here for a reason. It is a worthy exercise to go into your body and explore what no and yes feel like.

Go right now inside your body to that still quiet place that feels like your center and ask, "What does 'no' feel like in my body?" Really feel that. Now, "What does 'yes' feel like in your body?" Feel that deeply. Use these feelings the next time you're faced with a decision. You know what no and yes feel like in your body so you can go inside, ask the question of yourself and feel the answer. Feel the yes or the no that your body is telling you. It won't ever steer you wrong.

Bottom line: no is an important state of being. Like the story of forgiveness earlier in this book, saying no is a form of taking care of yourself and can open up the space for a yes.

"A 'No' uttered from deepest conviction is better and greater than a 'Yes' merely uttered to please, or what is worse, to avoid trouble."
- Mahatma Gandi

The Consistency Theory

People are nothing if not consistent in their behavior.

At some point it becomes our responsibility to behave differently from what we know will undoubtedly be our loved one's, friend's, colleague's consistent reaction to life's situations. They will likely react the same each time, but you don't have to.

"They always tell me what I can't do."

It doesn't matter; you know your potential.

"They get mad and yell when I am late, when I am early, when I breathe." It doesn't matter; your timing and your being are perfect just as they are. Others' perceptions are theirs and have no impact on you....unless you let them.

The Consistency Theory

Most people are consistent in their responses, to a fault. When you tell your parents something about your life, you pretty much know how they are going to respond, right? It's like that friend who is constantly victimized by similar events, then calls you offering the same complaints and emotions. How about that boss, who will likely be hypercritical no matter what you deliver to him. He will always find fault.

You can generally predict within a narrow percentage how someone that you work with, play with or have lived with, will react. At this point, it becomes your responsibility to find a new way to respond to their reaction. Now, knowing what your boss or parent will say, why would you tell them something that will generate a guaranteed negative response? Or even better, knowing that they will react a certain way no matter what you do, why would you continue to be upset by that?

I used to say about some people I had to have regular interactions with, who were totally consistent in their behavior, "I am shocked that I am shocked." With those people I decided there was a new way to deal with them, namely, don't. Don't get upset, don't react to their reaction, take a step back and recalibrate. Is this really upsetting or is this just habit? Does their reaction to what I am telling them have anything at all to do with me? Is it just them being them?

In most cases the answer to that last question is yes, it is just them acting the way they always have. You are not here to change them. Your job is to change your response to them. This shift in perspective can truly change your life. You don't ever have to be bothered by that person's consistent reactions to life again, you just let them be them.

What if no one is ever misbehaving...including you? - Alison Armstrong

Here are a couple of tricks to manage The Consistency Theory:

- The moment they go into their typically consistent reaction, gauge what you are feeling. See if you can step back and objectively look at their behavior as not being about you. Instead, see it as nothing more than a longstanding, habitual projection that this individual projects onto most of the people that he or she interacts with.

- Look at what this person is reflecting back to you. Take a moment and review if you have ever reacted to another human being in the same way this person is reacting to you. Take responsibility for your similar past behavior and forgive yourself, acknowledge yourself, love yourself and thank the universe for bringing this person to you to show you what you are ready to release. Even feel gratitude for the opportunity to grow, if you can.

- When in full engagement with this person and their reaction, change the subject. Get them off the downward spiral of reaction. This one works every time and there is no harm done to anyone. It just dissipates the energy.

Life's challenges either
s t i c k
to you or they don't.
If they
s t i c k
it's an opportunity to look
at it and take action.
It's all good. It's all you.

Photo by: Terri Graham

The Truth...What is That?

The path to the truth is a lifelong journey through judgment and back to the truth.

We experience the truth from our unique perspective of the world. One person's truth could be another person's lie. The truth can also be somewhat malleable, especially if life's lessons force us to change our minds. Through life's challenges and lessons, the angle of our perception can change, and what we thought was the truth might actually adjust with circumstances.

The diagram above is an illustration of these variances of "the truth." Our lives can be seen as journeys from judgment to truth and back to judgment again. We judge. That is what we as human beings do. Animals and plants don't judge in the same way humans do; they just "are." We judge in many ways. We declare, "The sky is blue" or "Your skin is a different color" or "That dog is a dog." We can

also assess and judge the events or relationships we experience as "positive" or "negative."

Those less positive judgments might lead us into darker emotions and even create fear, eventually moving us away from the truth, or they might move us back to a new version of the truth we are ready to experience.

The idea is that we constantly move from judgment to what we may experience as the truth at that moment, and then back to judgment. More importantly, that movement is life in its own cycle of creation and destruction, involution and evolution, expansion and contraction. When we find "the truth," that version of the truth then becomes the platform from which we view the world. That truth leads us to

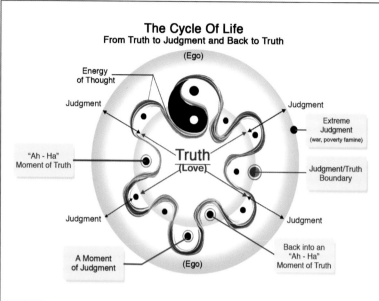

compare and contrast, which in itself is inherently a judgment, and the process circles around upon itself.

The opportunity is to use these moments of life to move through to the next stage. Look through the potential judgment and see that there is something more wonderful on the horizon that you may never have thought possible. Use it, it is all there for you.

"Life is a an experiential adventure providing moments of contrast, always taking us closer to our truth." – Jennifer McLean

You are the **spark**
You are the glint of the divine
All of us are ONE

"All that Is," is within each one of us

Life is there to **excite**, ignite,
create, **rekindle,** reflect, trigger,
mirror, reveal, show and **expose**
to, through and around us

Be the vessel for **love** in the world

Darkness is You, As is the Light

The process of letting judgments go is similar to moving from the light to the dark; it is the yin and yang process. From this perspective, it can be said that darkness is you, as is the light. Through the light we become aware that there is darkness. The borders of the dark become a landmark or a contrast to see and align with the light and reflect to us what living in the light means. In essence, one can't understand what the light is unless there is darkness to make the light known.

Similarly, judgment in its negative sense is the juxtaposition of the truth with something we see or experience, and the lessons of judgment can actually lead us back to the truth. It is a necessary piece of the puzzle. You know what you want by contrasting it to what you don't want. It is judgment and fear that create the chains that bind us. However, if we understand that judgment, and the fears that arise out of that judgment, are useful and can assist us in finding healing for old unresolved issues, we can live a life that has more faith, light and trust. Eventually we have the opportunity to explore our judgments and fears without moving too far away from the truth, our truth.

Each time we explore our individual perspectives of the world we have the choice to stay closer to the "boundary of truth" (as illustrated in the diagram on page 63) or move further into judgment. It is creative extremism; it takes a creative exploration into the extreme reaches of judgment or darkness in order to find a middle ground or, better yet, the extreme reaches of happiness.

Both birth and death are transitions. Whether a human being passes or the season of Summer "dies" to Fall, these transitions deliver the cycle of life and the cycle of creation. Not one part of that cycle is wrong or bad. It simply is.

Here again there can be judgment attached to creative moments of change, but the truth remains that life passages are a part of us. When these moments of change are truly examined, they cannot be judged, but reviewed and accepted as opportunities to feel more deeply, evolve further, grow stronger, learn more and live more authentically. They become further opportunities to find the next iteration of our individual truths.

Criticism often reflects what you feel about yourself. Criticism makes victims. If you can turn away from negative thoughts and feelings of victimization, to trust the patterns of life, you might discover a new dimension of thinking. Remember, what is occurring around you is the divine dance of natural law. If you have a judgment to make about the happenings around you, then use those observations and the resulting feelings to make new discoveries about yourself and the nature of the world around you.

Make an effort to seek out the truth as a litmus test to determine whether your judgments are real. If you are making judgments about global or political issues, use that energy to propel yourself to be a model of integrity, love and peace. Buy a hybrid car, help someone in need get back on their feet, find a spiritual center, participate. Reflect the highest levels of positive energy back into the appearance of chaos.

"When you love God, and when you see God in every soul, you cannot be mean." - Paramahansa Yogananda

Special Thanks
A special thanks to the artists! The photography and artwork was contributed by artists from all over the world:

Fiona Almeleh (South Africa) - "Painting Light" page 8
Fiona has been facilitating creative exploration and healing through color and art for the past sixteen years and works as an energy intuitive, healer, artist, author and teacher. Fiona's art has been exhibited both overseas and locally in South Africa. Some of these works may be viewed on the Galleries page of her website www.fionaalmeleh.com

Joao Pãglione (Germany) - "Moon Tree" page 12 and "Sundown" page 40
"Maestro de nada, aprendiz de to   do. When I read that phrase in Spanish (it means "A Master of Nothing, Apprentice of All") I realized it described my life and what I had done and was searching for. Photography is for me a constant discovery and rediscovery of the realization of my environment, the beauty surrounding me, and how I envision it. It allows me to explore other people's world and portray those worlds to other people. It's my true passion and self-realization. Click."

Katy L. Zahner (USA) - Little Girls page 14
Katy Zahner has enjoyed her life as an artist for the last 60 years. Her medium has always been oil. Katy attended Fontbonne Art Institute in St. Louis and the Kansas City Art Institute. Katy took the photograph and then painted it because the expressions on the girls intrigued her. Katy's grandaughter Laura was expressing joy at receiving the rose and her friend Ashley had an opposite expression of jealousy.

Roger Bloom (USA) - "Katie and Rev. David" page 22
Roger Bloom is a former journalist and current marketing and PR consultant who lives in Huntington Beach, California. He can be reached via roger@rogerbloom.com. He would like to dedicate this work to the memory of Katie (in the picture), whose irrepressible spirit lives on in the hearts of everyone who loved her, and to Rev. David Phears, Senior Minister of Sangha Spiritual Center.

Richard Wanderman (USA) - "The Pitcher" page 27
"My wife Anne picked this pitcher up at a tag sale over thirty years ago. It's amazing that the handle has lived through kids growing up, countless visitors, cats, dogs, and everything else that goes on in busy households. The body of the pitcher is quite solid but a handle with the bottom unattached is beautiful and functional and vulnerable. We use it for milk and at times for maple syrup."
Richard has a BFA and an MFA in Fine and Applied Arts from the University of Oregon where he studied ceramics, design, and photography and taught ceramics, basic design, and computer applications for artists. rwanderman.com

Alexander Gobell (USA) - "Dawn Passion" page 28
Alex is a lifelong amateur photographer who has mainly taken the obligatory family photos. Now in retirement he has found Flickr, which has given him the impetus to photograph whatever delights his eye. Not surprisingly this usually involves the magic of the light. http://www.flickr.com/photos/algo/

James Chiou (Taiwan) - "Sunflowers at Sunset" page 30
James' thought about sunflowers at sunset: "Think bright, and believe the most powerful strength in the world lies within your heart." http://www.flickr.com/photos/chieftain-y/

Aimee Rousseau (USA) - "Butterfly" page 34
Aimee Rousseau's paintings carry a vibrational frequency or signature that can heal the viewer in different ways. Her watercolors are painted using Blue Solar Water and divine inspiration as the Ho'oponopono prayer runs steadily through her mind. Ho'oponopono is the ancient Hawaiian art of making things right. This powerful prayer is a tool for neutralizing and purifying the things we see, feel and experience that we don't resonate with. It releases the ancient, as well as the fresh, energy of the thoughts and memories that cause life imbalances, pain and disease. www.healingpainting.com

Michael Ringer (USA) - "Adirondack Silence" page 36
Michael's paintings and sculptures are in collections worldwide. Eight books have been published on his art. Michael's home is on the St. Lawrence River a short distance from the Adirondacks, in New York. The painting "Adirondack Silence" seen in this book is a scene of Bald Mountain Pond near Old Forge, N.Y. in the heart of the Adirondack Mountains. More of his work can be seen at www.michaelringer.com
Keith and Maura Leon (USA) - Song lyrics "I Am The Light" page 31
The song "I Am The Light" was written by Keith and Maura Leon, co-owners of Successful Communications, Inc. and co-authors of, The Seven Steps to Successful Relationships. To learn more about this inspirational couple visit: www.relationship-masters.com

Ruth Savitz (USA) - "Housecat Dreams: Forest Cat" page 42
Ruth's photograph shows a lovely pet looking out the window of his home at Fitler Square Park in Philadelphia, Pennsylvania. The photo combines several of Ruth's favorite subjects: animals, nature, and the charming sites of Philadelphia. http://www.photosofphiladelphia.com/, http://flickr.com/photos/moocat/

Flávio Cruvinel Brandão (Brazil) - "Swallow-tailed Hummingbird" page 44
Economist, father and husband, Flávio is an avid nature photographer with a penchant for the feathered. This wonderful Hummingbird is called Swallow-tailed Hummingbird (Eupetomena macroura), Beija-flor tesoura in Portuguese, because it has a forked tail. Its green body and blue/purple head become iridescent, depending on the light.
It's common in the Brazilin cities, like Brasília, the capital of Brazil. This bird is territorial and aggressive if others birds invade its area. http://www.flickr.com/photos/flaviocb/

Denzil Fernandes (England) - "Playing with Fire" page 54
Denzil Fernandes is currently a teacher of Biology in a high school in Cambridge, England. His passion for photography has only blossomed in recent years and he thoroughly enjoys finding the occasional moment, when not at work or with his loving wife, to capture an interesting image or two. This photo was taken of his sister-in-law (Esther) playing with fire-poi during a late summer evening at a party in the South of France. http://www.flickr.com/photos/denzil/

Dan Canavan (Australia) - "Me and My Shadow" page 56
Dan Canavan was born in Melbourne, Australia in 1927. An accountant, Dan was married with four children. He was a foundation member of the Preston Photographic Club in a northern suburb of Melbourne from 1948 until his death in 2006. Dan won every club award, some of them several times.
Dan was one of the photographic art's true gentlemen, always willing to advise and assist new photographers to improve their skills and enjoy photography. Dan's forte was Land/Seascape, but he was also proficient at the grab shot, as illustrated by the one he called "Me and My Shadow".

Malcolm Brown (Canada) - "NO" page 59
Malcolm Brown is an international award winning GRAPHIC designer in addition to being a STRONG, OLD-SCHOOL, MULTI-MEDIA artist. "NO" was INCLUDED IN an exhibition (3 YEARS OF GOD & GOO) CONSISTING of 33 paintings, combining layered imagery, large overt texts and scratchy penciled slogans. Iconic, ironic, terribly true and all about 'the DAILY instants' that happen every instant. The painting 'NO' forces pause and reflection before clear-headed action TAKES PLACE. www.supercrasher.ca

Helene Barbara (USA) "With Grace and Ease" page 60
Helene Barbara lives in California. Helene's photographic artwork is an expression of Nature's beauty combined with the fascinating experience of our human lives. In the lotus flower image, titled "With Grace and Ease", one can see in the world of Nature, the loveliness of a life lived with Inner Peace and Natural Harmony. www.printroom.com/pro/simplynatural

Terri Graham (USA) - "Bee" page 62
"My art is an extension and expression of who I am spiritually. I endeavor to show the profound impact that the love of Jesus the Christ has had in my life."